# DESTINATION:
# PLANET
# EARTH

## WIDE EYED EDITIONS

# The Oceans and Continents

Let's travel to places even the most daring explorers can't reach, from deep under the Earth's crust to high up in its atmosphere. We'll discover what makes our planet so dynamic and bursting with life—and why it's so fragile.

From space, planet Earth looks like a big blue marble. That's because almost three-quarters of its surface is covered in water. The rest is land, divided up into seven large landmasses called continents, with thousands of smaller islands sprinkled in between.

## Blue Planet

Around 97% of Earth's water is in its seas and oceans. Less than 1% of the water on Earth is FRESHWATER, the non-salty water found in lakes, rivers, and glaciers. There is really only ONE WORLD OCEAN, but it's subdivided into five large sections.

The five oceans are the Pacific, the Atlantic, the Indian, the Arctic, and the Southern oceans. Then there are smaller bodies of saltwater where the land and oceans meet, known as SEAS.

### The Surface of the Earth

Freshwater
Land
Saltwater

## Underwater Life

Water makes up an incredible 99% OF OUR PLANET'S LIVING SPACE. On land, there's life from a few feet underground to the tops of the trees, but in the ocean there's life at every level, from the water's surface to the deepest parts of the ocean. And they're very deep—up to 7.5 miles.

North America

Atlantic Ocean

Africa

Pacific Ocean

South America

Southern Ocean

Antarctic

## The Big Seven

The SEVEN CONTINENTS aren't actually huge separate islands. Narrow strips of land, known as isthmuses, join North America to South America and Africa to Asia, while Europe and Asia form one large landmass, known as Eurasia. The other two continents are much more separate—Antarctica at the very south of the planet, and the smallest continent, Australia.

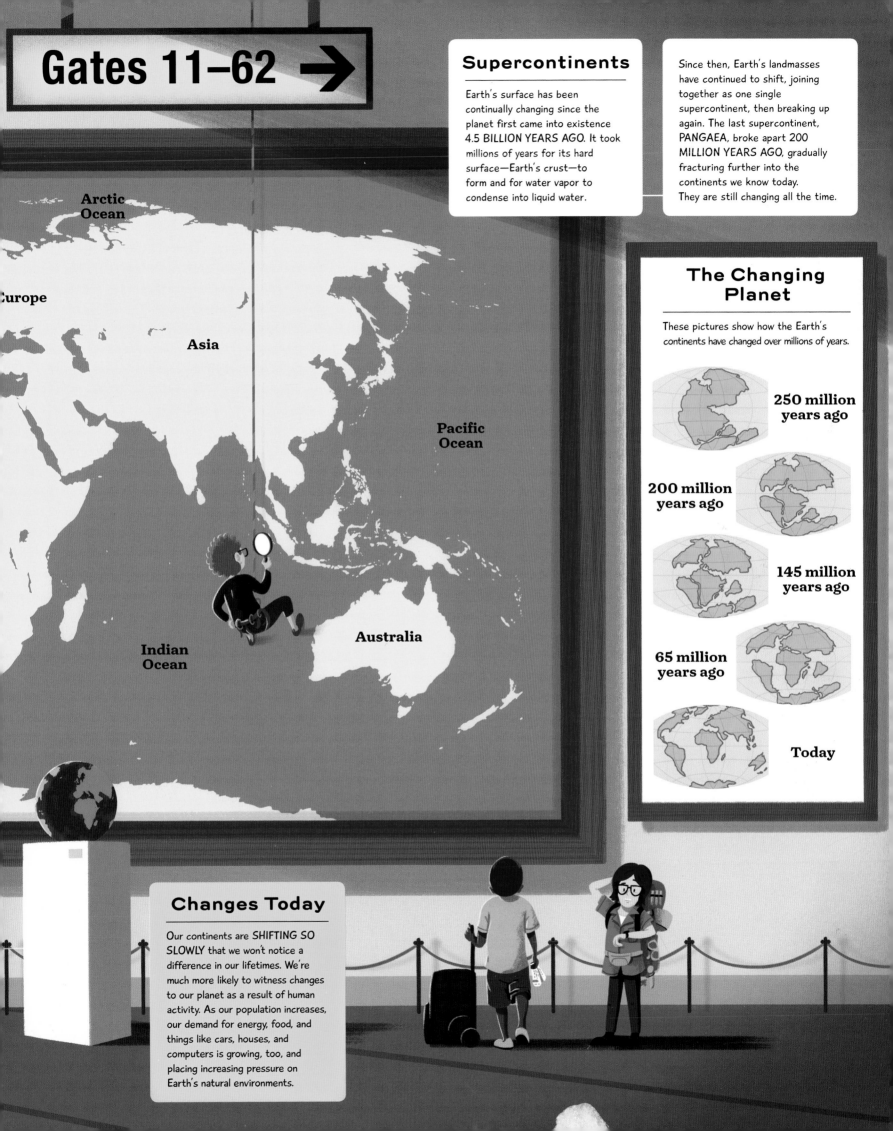

# Gates 11–62 →

**Arctic Ocean**

Europe

**Asia**

**Pacific Ocean**

**Indian Ocean**

**Australia**

## Supercontinents

Earth's surface has been continually changing since the planet first came into existence 4.5 BILLION YEARS AGO. It took millions of years for its hard surface—Earth's crust—to form and for water vapor to condense into liquid water.

Since then, Earth's landmasses have continued to shift, joining together as one single supercontinent, then breaking up again. The last supercontinent, PANGAEA, broke apart 200 MILLION YEARS AGO, gradually fracturing further into the continents we know today. They are still changing all the time.

## The Changing Planet

These pictures show how the Earth's continents have changed over millions of years.

**250 million years ago**

**200 million years ago**

**145 million years ago**

**65 million years ago**

**Today**

## Changes Today

Our continents are SHIFTING SO SLOWLY that we won't notice a difference in our lifetimes. We're much more likely to witness changes to our planet as a result of human activity. As our population increases, our demand for energy, food, and things like cars, houses, and computers is growing, too, and placing increasing pressure on Earth's natural environments.

# Navigating the World

We can pinpoint exactly where we are in the world and find our way to even the most far-flung places thanks to accurate maps and sophisticated satellite technology.

This wasn't always the case. For thousands of years, people thought the world was flat. Europeans didn't travel to America until 1492, or Australia until 1606! For hundreds of years, daring explorers journeyed into the unknown—literally—making the first maps of the places they discovered. Their heroic efforts, coupled with recent advances in technology, mean we now have a much more detailed picture of the world.

## Guiding Stars

Before compasses and satellites, travelers used the stars to find their way. In the northern hemisphere, you can use Polaris, also known as the North Star, to find north—this star always remains directly above the North Pole. In the southern hemisphere, the Southern Cross constellation can help you figure out which way south is.

## Using Satellites

Today we can use a GPS (Global Positioning System) receiver to determine our exact position. The receiver locates four or more satellites in the sky above, calculates the distance to each one, and uses this information to deduce its own location. Many cars and most smartphones have this feature, to help you find your way around.

## Where Am I?

Maps give 2-D drawings of an area, with symbols and shading to represent different features. Each map has a key to explain the meaning of the shading.

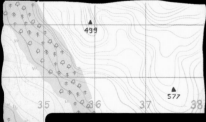

Geographical maps highlight Earth's natural features, such as mountains and valleys.

Political maps show the borders between nations.

This map shows how many people live in each area.

## Latitude and Longitude

Every place on Earth has a global address, which is given as two numbers called COORDINATES. The first number tells you how far east or west the place is, and the second number tells you how far north or south it is. We measure coordinates in degrees, using imaginary lines called latitude and longitude.

LATITUDE and LONGITUDE divide the globe into strips and segments. Latitude lines run horizontally, in belts around the planet. Longitude lines (known as meridians) run vertically, from pole to pole. The starting point for latitude is the EQUATOR, the imaginary central band around the Earth. For longitude, the starting point is an imaginary vertical line that goes through Greenwich in London, England, known as the PRIME MERIDIAN.

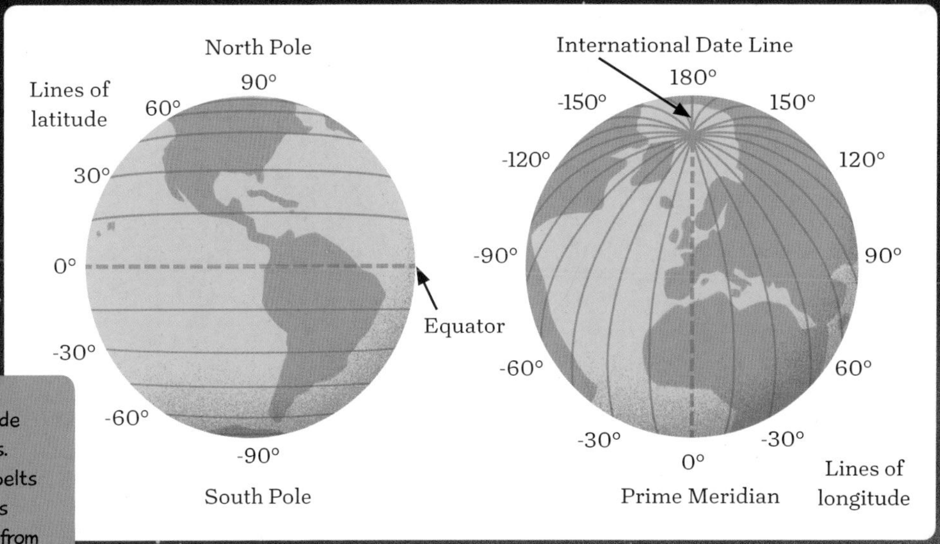

North Pole
90°
Lines of latitude
60°
30°
0°
-30°
-60°
-90°
South Pole

Equator

International Date Line
180°
-150°
150°
-120°
120°
-90°
90°
-60°
60°
-30°
-30°
0°
Prime Meridian

Lines of longitude

## Time and Place

Lines of longitude mark the DIFFERENCE IN TIME from one place to the next, starting from the Prime Meridian in Greenwich. The time gets an hour later for every 15 degrees farther west you go...until you meet the International Date Line, on the opposite side of the Earth from Greenwich, in the middle of the Pacific Ocean. Then you skip forward a whole 24 hours!

# The Poles

**Travel as far north or as far south as you can and you'll reach the North or South Pole—but don't expect to find a big pole there.**

The poles are imaginary. They represent the two ends of the Earth's axis—the imaginary line around which the Earth moves. The planet spins around once every 24 hours, which is why a day is 24 hours long. In that time, most places on Earth experience light and darkness—day and night—but this isn't the case at the poles. Earth's axis is at a tilt, so the very top and the very bottom only experience one sunrise and one sunset a year. They have six months of daylight and six months of darkness!

## A Tilting Planet

As well as spinning on its axis daily, the Earth also MOVES AROUND THE SUN. Because the Earth spins on a tilt, the North Pole is tipped away from the Sun for half the year and tipped toward the Sun for the other half of the year. The opposite is true for the South Pole. The Earth's tilt gives us our SEASONS. When it's summer in the northern hemisphere (the part of the world above the equator), it's winter in the southern hemisphere (below the equator) and vice versa.

The Earth takes just over 365 days to orbit (move around) the Sun. That's why a year is 365 DAYS LONG.

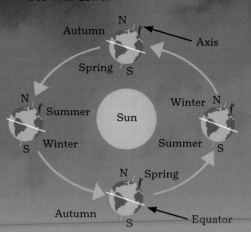

## The North Pole

The NORTH POLE is located in the middle of the Arctic Ocean, where the sea's surface has been frozen for millions of years. This frozen ice cap is home to polar bears, seals, and birds, while whales and Arctic fish swim underneath.

## Melting Ice Caps

The polar ice caps get bigger over the long winter months, as more sea freezes over, and melt back during the warmer summer months.

Recently, however, an increase in the average global temperature has caused the ice caps to SHRINK. With more sea ice melting, sea levels across the globe are gradually beginning to rise, threatening to flood low-lying coastal areas.

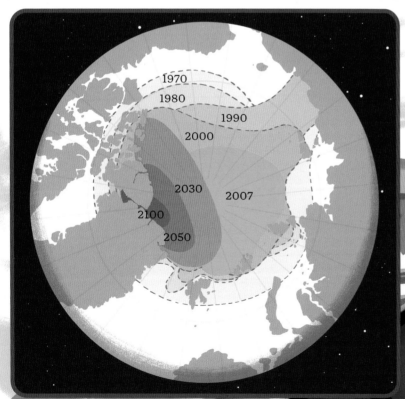

This diagram shows how dramatically the ice caps have shrunk since 1970 in the Arctic. As you can see, if the planet continues to heat up at its current rate, they will have almost disappeared by 2100.

## The South Pole

The SOUTH POLE is located on the vast, frozen land mass of Antarctica. It's one of the coldest place on Earth, with temperatures reaching below -100° Fahrenheit. Even the hardiest penguins don't come this far inland. The only living beings are researchers at the Amundsen-Scott research station.

## Ice Core Samples

Researchers collect samples of ice that formed tens of thousands of years ago to examine how the world has changed over the years. Through studying bubbles trapped in the ice, scientists can tell which gases used to make up the Earth's atmosphere, and how warm the planet used to be.

>> Roald Amundsen    >> Robert F. Scott

## Intrepid Explorers

The Amundsen-Scott research station is named after the first two explorers to reach the South Pole: Norwegian ROALD AMUNDSEN and British officer ROBERT F. SCOTT.

Amundsen and his team reached the pole in December 1911, a month ahead of Scott. On the return journey, Scott and his men sadly perished from the extreme cold.

# The Equator

**Need to thaw out after a long winter in Antarctica? Head as far away from the poles as is possible on Earth: the Equator.**

This vast, imaginary belt around the Earth's middle divides the northern half of the globe, known as the northern hemisphere, from the southern half—the southern hemisphere. Along the Equator, the Sun's rays are at their most direct—the Sun passes straight overhead—and the Earth's tilt has little effect on the temperature or length of day, so there aren't really seasons.

## Follow the Sun

SUNRISES and SUNSETS are quicker along the Equator than elsewhere on Earth—it takes just a few minutes for day to turn into night. The Sun appears at roughly 6 a.m. and sets at roughly 6 p.m. every day of the year.

Twice a year the Sun is directly above the Equator: on March 20 or 21 and September 22 or 23. These days are known as the Equinoxes, and at noon on the Equator, a stick pointing straight up will cast no shadow at all.

## Hot and Humid

It never gets cold at the Equator, but it's not always sunny. The hot sun continually EVAPORATES water from the ocean, which falls back down as heavy rain. This warm, wet weather is ideal for RAIN FORESTS, where animals and plants thrive.

Rain forests cover just 2% of the Earth's surface—mostly around the Equator—but they're home to MORE THAN HALF of the planet's species of plants and animals.

## The Power of Spin

As the Earth spins, three interesting things happen at the Equator.

1. The spinning force makes the middle BULGE OUT, so the Earth is wider at the Equator than it is at the poles.

2. The force of GRAVITY (which pulls things toward Earth) becomes a little weaker.

3. The Earth's surface TRAVELS FASTER at the Equator than it does at the rest of the globe— because it's wider at the Equator, it has farther to go to complete a full rotation in 24 hours.

Space agencies often launch spacecraft from locations near the Equator. The bulge means they're a bit closer to space, weaker gravity means there's less force to push against, and the extra speed gives their takeoff more oomph!

**Earth**

Spin

Equator

The widest part of the planet spins fastest

The narrower parts of the planet spin more slowly

# The Atmosphere

**The Earth is surrounded by a blanket of gases we call the atmosphere. Without it, we wouldn't be here.**

The universe is a dangerous place. Stars give out harmful rays, meteors collide with planets, and away from the heat given off by stars, it can be absolutely freezing. We need our atmosphere to protect us. We also depend on oxygen and water in the atmosphere to survive. Without these vital ingredients, there would be very little life on Earth.

## Layers of Air

The ATMOSPHERE is held in place by GRAVITY—the Earth's pulling force—and is much thicker closer to Earth's surface, where the planet's gravity is greatest. The atmosphere extends up around 6,000 miles, thinning out along the way, to where tiny particles simply float off into space. It's divided roughly into FIVE LAYERS. Explore them below!

2. The **stratosphere** is where planes fly above the clouds and there's an important layer of gas called ozone.

1. The **troposphere** is where our weather happens.

The air is mostly made up of the gases NITROGEN (78%) and OXYGEN (21%). Other gases include water vapor, carbon dioxide, methane, nitrous oxide, and ozone.

## Greenhouse Effect

Like glass on a greenhouse, our ATMOSPHERE lets heat from the Sun in but stops too much from escaping. Without this greenhouse effect, Earth's heat would escape into space and we would all freeze.

In recent years, humans have added more greenhouse gases to the atmosphere—in particular CARBON DIOXIDE—by burning fossil fuels (coal, oil, and gas) and cutting down forests, which store carbon dioxide. Because there are more gases to trap the Sun's heat, our planet is gradually warming up.

## Protection From Space

The Sun and other stars emit all kinds of HARMFUL RAYS: cosmic rays, gamma rays, X-rays, ultra-violet (UV) rays...Fortunately our atmosphere acts like a barrier and stops most of them from reaching Earth.

The OZONE LAYER is particularly important for blocking out UV rays, which can damage our skin and eyes. Then there's the threat of meteors, comets, and other space debris colliding with Earth. Again, our atmosphere comes to the rescue by burning up most objects before they can reach us.

5. The **exosphere** is where satellites are sent to orbit the Earth.

4. The **thermosphere** is where space officially begins. This is where the International Space Station orbits the Earth.

3. The **mesosphere** is the coldest part, only accessible by rocket.

>> Why does it get colder as I get closer to the Sun?

Because the Sun heats up the Earth and the Earth warms the air above it. The higher you go, the thinner the air and the less heat it can hold.

## The Great Oxidation Event

We have tiny blue-green algae to thank for the existence of oxygen in our atmosphere. For the first half of planet Earth's history, there was no oxygen. Then these microscopic organisms evolved and began using a process called PHOTOSYNTHESIS to make their food. They took sunshine and carbon dioxide from the atmosphere and turned them into energy for themselves. They released oxygen back into the atmosphere as a waste product. Eventually, around 2.45 BILLION YEARS AGO, there were enough algae giving off oxygen for it to become a major gas in our atmosphere.

# Weather

**Wouldn't it be great if you could control the weather? You could make sure it never rained on your birthday and it could snow whenever you wanted a day off from school!**

The right weather at the right time has been crucial throughout history for growing and harvesting crops. People have even performed rain and sun dances to try to get the weather they wanted. But predicting the weather is tricky, and controlling it is virtually impossible.

## Making Weather

The SUN is the main cause of all our weather. As well as giving us sunny days, it also creates wind and causes clouds to form. AIR and WATER both play an important part too.

When one large area of air warms up more than another, it starts to move and that's what creates WIND. When the Sun heats up the oceans, lots of water droplets gather in the sky and that's what creates CLOUDS.

STRATUS CLOUDS are like long, low sheets that seem to cover the entire sky.

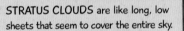

ALTOCUMULUS and ALTOSTRATUS CLOUDS hover at medium height.

CIRRUS CLOUDS are high and wispy. They're made of ice crystals.

CUMULONIMBUS CLOUDS are storm clouds that stretch high into the sky.

CUMULUS CLOUDS are the low, fluffy ones.

NIMBOSTRATUS CLOUDS are dark sheets of cloud that bring drizzle.

## Clouds

Clouds form when the Sun heats water on Earth. The water rises up as a gas, then cools and turns into water droplets, floating in the air. Clouds are groups of water droplets that have clustered together. Fluffy white clouds and high, wispy clouds appear on sunny days, while thick, low sheets of clouds and towering dark thunderclouds mean you're in for some rain.

In freezing cold weather, tiny crystals of ice gather together and fall as SNOW. In big storm clouds, water droplets are driven high into the sky, where they freeze and then fall as HAILSTONES.

## Extreme Weather

When the weather gets really bad, it can severely disrupt people's lives. Heavy downpours may lead to the FLOODING of roads, railway lines, and homes. Long periods of hot sun may lead to DROUGHTS, when crops can't grow, animals can't graze, and people can go hungry. BLIZZARDS are heavy snowstorms that can cut off towns and villages until the snow is finally cleared. As the world warms up, we're experiencing more extreme weather than in the past. Warmer seas and air mean more water droplets in the sky, creating larger storm clouds. The clouds get so heavy that rain or snow falls suddenly in one area, while other areas may receive no rain at all.

## Weather Forecasts

How do weather forecasters know what the weather will be like tomorrow? They don't know for sure—they make guesses. They measure what's going on in the atmosphere, compare their results with what's happened in the past, and look for patterns to suggest what might happen in the future. Here are some of the instruments they use:

A WIND SOCK measures wind direction (the way it's pointing shows you the way the wind is blowing) and wind speed (the higher the speed, the more horizontal the sock).

A THERMOMETER measures the temperature.

A BAROMETER measures air pressure—how much the air is pushing down on the Earth. If the pressure falls, then you're in for stormy, wet weather. If the pressure rises, it's likely to be sunny and dry.

A RAIN GAUGE measures how much rain falls over a certain time.

## Wind

Winds can be light and breezy or strong enough to blow a house down. They're rated from 0 to 12 on a scale known as the BEAUFORT SCALE. The higher the number, the faster the wind speed—and the higher the likelihood of something getting blown over!

# Climate

How does the weather where you live change from month to month and through the year? While the daily weather forecast can be hard to predict, overall weather patterns are usually much more reliable. The typical, long-term weather pattern for an area is called its climate.

Climates vary greatly around the world, from the icy polar regions, where hurricane winds blow, through dry continental (inland) areas, chilly mountains and mild coastlines, to tropical climates near the Equator, where it's hot and rainy nearly every day.

These different climates are mainly caused by the uneven way the Sun heats up the Earth's surface. The temperature difference between the Equator and the poles sets off powerful flows of cold and warm air, known as air currents. These currents determine which way the wind blows and where your weather comes from. How high up you live and how far you are from the sea also make a big difference in the climate you're likely to experience.

## Climate Zones

The POLAR ZONES are the areas around the North and South Poles that are always partly covered in ice. They never have warm summers.

In the TEMPERATE ZONES, next to the Polar zones, the climate is neither baking hot nor freezing cold. Here you are more likely to experience four distinct seasons—spring, summer, autumn, and winter.

If you want a snowy winter, head for the mountains. If you want a dry, warm summer, try the Mediterranean coast or the west coast of America.

The TROPICAL ZONE around the equator, with its wet rain forests and dry deserts, is hot all year round.

## Oceans and Continents

Oceans heat up more slowly than landmasses, but once water is warm, it keeps its heat for much longer than land. That's why areas by the sea tend to have MILDER WINTERS and COOLER SUMMERS. By contrast, areas in the middle of continents have much more EXTREME SEASONS. Summer in northern Asia, for example, can be as hot as 86° Fahrenheit while the temperature in winter can plummet to -22° Fahrenheit.

## Adapting to Climates

People all over the world have adapted their lives to suit the climate they live in. For example:

Wearing long, loose, light-colored clothes in hot countries can help to keep you cool.

Building well-insulated homes in cold countries can keep you warm.

In many hot countries, people stop work for a couple of hours over the hottest part of the day and even have a siesta (a short afternoon nap). They've then got the energy to get more jobs done later in the day, when the weather is cooler.

## Wet and Dry

Tropical RAIN FORESTS around the equator are WARM AND WET throughout the year, but travel inland a little farther north or south, and you'll find the planet's HOTTEST, DRIEST CLIMATES. The rain has already fallen over forests, coasts, and mountain areas, leaving these areas to bake in the Sun and turn into vast DESERTS such as the Sahara and the Kalahari.

Some tropical areas have a mixed wet-dry climate, with a wet season, when all their rain falls, and a dry season, when there's no rain at all. Herds of zebra, elephants, and other animals go on long journeys during the dry season, in search of rivers or water holes.

## Climate Change

Throughout our planet's history, its climate has been changing. There have been colder periods, known as ICE AGES, and warmer periods with no ice at all. An ice age is when sheets of ice cover some of the Earth, so we're still in an Ice Age now. The ice is melting though, and for the first time in history, humans are at least partly responsible for the planet getting warmer.

# Ecosystems

There are over two million different species of living things—or organisms—on planet Earth. They rely on each other and their environments to survive, in an interconnected network known as an ecosystem.

An ecosystem can be as small as a garden pond or as large as a forest. The things living in it can range from the tiniest organisms, invisible to the human eye, to the tallest trees, standing over 300 feet high. Every organism has a role to play in its ecosystem. So do environmental conditions, such as sunlight and water. The arrival of a new organism or a change in the environment can threaten to destroy an ecosystem.

## Food Chains

All organisms need ENERGY to grow, move, and reproduce. For an ecosystem to work well, there needs to be a flow of energy within it. PLANTS and ALGAE get energy from the Sun, HERBIVOROUS ANIMALS get energy by feeding on plants, and CARNIVOROUS ANIMALS get energy by feeding on animals. This sequence is called a food chain. There are many possible combinations for food chains in an ecosystem.

## Extreme Habitats

Organisms have adapted to live in nearly every corner of the Earth, even under the most extreme conditions. Deep under the ocean, far away from any sunlight, are cracks in the ocean floor that emit poisonous gases and boiling hot water. These are known as HYDROTHERMAL VENTS. Astonishingly, bacteria have adapted to survive in the vents and provide food for other life-forms, such as giant tube worms, clams, and shrimp!

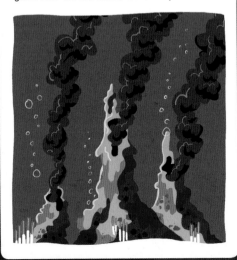

## Producers

The food chain in a pond begins with pond weed and algae. They're known as PRODUCERS because they produce their own food from the Sun's light.

## Food Pyramids

Food chains are sometimes shown as a pyramid, because there are many more plants than herbivores and many more herbivores than carnivores.

**Tertiary consumers** eat secondary consumers

**Secondary consumers** eat primary consumers

**Primary consumers** eat producers

**Producers** make energy from the Sun

## Top Consumer

In this pond ecosystem, the heron bird is the TOP CONSUMER, because no one else dares to eat it. There's a predator like the heron at the top of every food chain.

## Consumers

Insects, fish, frogs, and birds make up the next series of links in the food chain. They're known as the consumers. First the herbivores—the small insects and fish—consume (eat) the plants and algae. They're known as PRIMARY CONSUMERS. Then the carnivores—the larger fish, frogs, and birds—consume the herbivores. They're known as SECONDARY CONSUMERS. Predators that eat other carnivores are known as TERTIARY CONSUMERS.

## Decomposers

Bacteria and fungi are the final link in the food chain, turning it into more of a cycle. They DECOMPOSE (break down) dead plants and animals and turn them into soil... from which new plants can grow!

# Biomes

**Planet Earth can be divided into around ten extremely large types of ecosystems, known as biomes.**

The climate and geography of an area make it more suitable for some kinds of life-forms than others. Camels are most at home in hot, dry deserts, while banana plants need the heat and heavy rain found in tropical rain forests. Most biomes are named after the main vegetation of each area, such as rain forest or grassland, but deserts and tundra are named after their lack of vegetation—the word "tundra" comes from a Finnish word that means "flat, treeless land." The largest biome on Earth is the ocean—which isn't surprising, considering that water covers 71% of the planet. Let's explore the major biomes on land.

## Coniferous Forest

The planet's largest biome, apart from the oceans, is the vast band of coniferous forests that circles the globe, known as the TAIGA or BOREAL FOREST. Coniferous trees are trees that make pinecones and don't lose their leaves during the winter. The taiga contains a third of all the trees on Earth and stretches through North America, northern Europe, and much of northern Asia. It marks the northernmost area where trees can survive—winters are long and cold, with lots of snow, and the summers are very short. Animals are either seasonal visitors or extremely resourceful. Crossbill birds have found a way to survive through the winter by using their crossed beaks to pry open pinecones and eat the seeds inside.

## Temperate Deciduous Forest

DECIDUOUS TREES grow in temperate areas, where the weather is milder. There are four different seasons in temperate biomes—winter, spring, summer, and autumn—but it never gets very hot nor very cold. Unlike the thin pine needles of the coniferous evergreens, deciduous trees have broad, fleshy leaves. Through the warmer months, their leaves are excellent for collecting light to make the tree's food. They also make tasty snacks for animals, from tiny insects called aphids to large leaf-munching deer. They shed their leaves in autumn and remain dormant until spring.

## Grasslands

Grasslands develop in the middle of continents or beyond large mountain ranges—areas where there's not enough rainfall for forests to form. Hot tropical grasslands are also known as SAVANNAS. They're often found between rain forests and deserts, and they're home to many large animals, from elephants and zebras to lions and leopards. Temperate grasslands tend to be cooler and include the prairies of North America, the pampas of South America, and the steppes of Central Asia. Herds of antelopes and bison roam these areas, as well as wolves, wild dogs, and many smaller animals.

## Tropical or Temperate?

TROPICAL forests and grasslands occur near the Equator, where it's warm throughout the year. TEMPERATE forests and grasslands occur away from the Equator, where the climates are cooler and the seasons are more distinct.

## Desert

One fifth of the land on Earth is made up of DESERTS. They can be sandy or rocky, hot or cold—Antarctica is a desert—but they are all very dry. Only a few well-adapted plants and animals are able to survive in these areas. Snakes and scorpions stay cool by burrowing under the sand, while cactus plants have far-reaching roots to soak up any available water.

## Tundra

North of the taiga is the frozen, wind-swept, treeless tundra, the COLDEST OF ALL BIOMES, which circles the North Pole. Even fewer animals survive here, though you'll find polar bears, reindeer, and plenty of fish. In some places, the only plants are the mosses and lichen that cling to the bare rock.

# Water

Water might not seem very interesting, but without it, life on Earth would be impossible. All the water on Earth has been around for billions of years. Next time it rains, or you wash your hands under a tap, just think where else that water might have been over the centuries.

No other planet in the solar system has water in all three states (solid, liquid, and gas). Water is continually moving through these states in a process known as the water cycle. The water cycle is driven by the Sun's heat energy. Clouds, rain, rivers and the oceans are all part of the same continuous process.

## Condensation

Water vapor cools as it rises higher in the sky and condenses into tiny water droplets. The vapor releases heat as it changes from a gas state to a liquid, causing the droplets to waft up higher. When there are lots of water droplets in the sky, they group together as CLOUDS.

## Evaporation

Around 90% of the water in our atmosphere comes from the oceans, lakes, and rivers. The Sun's heat EVAPORATES surface water, turning it into an invisible gas called WATER VAPOR, which rises up with the warm air.

## Transpiration

About 10% of the water in our atmosphere comes from the leaves of plants. The plants suck water in from the soil through their roots and some of that water TRANSPIRES—comes out as water vapor—through tiny pores in the undersides of the leaves.

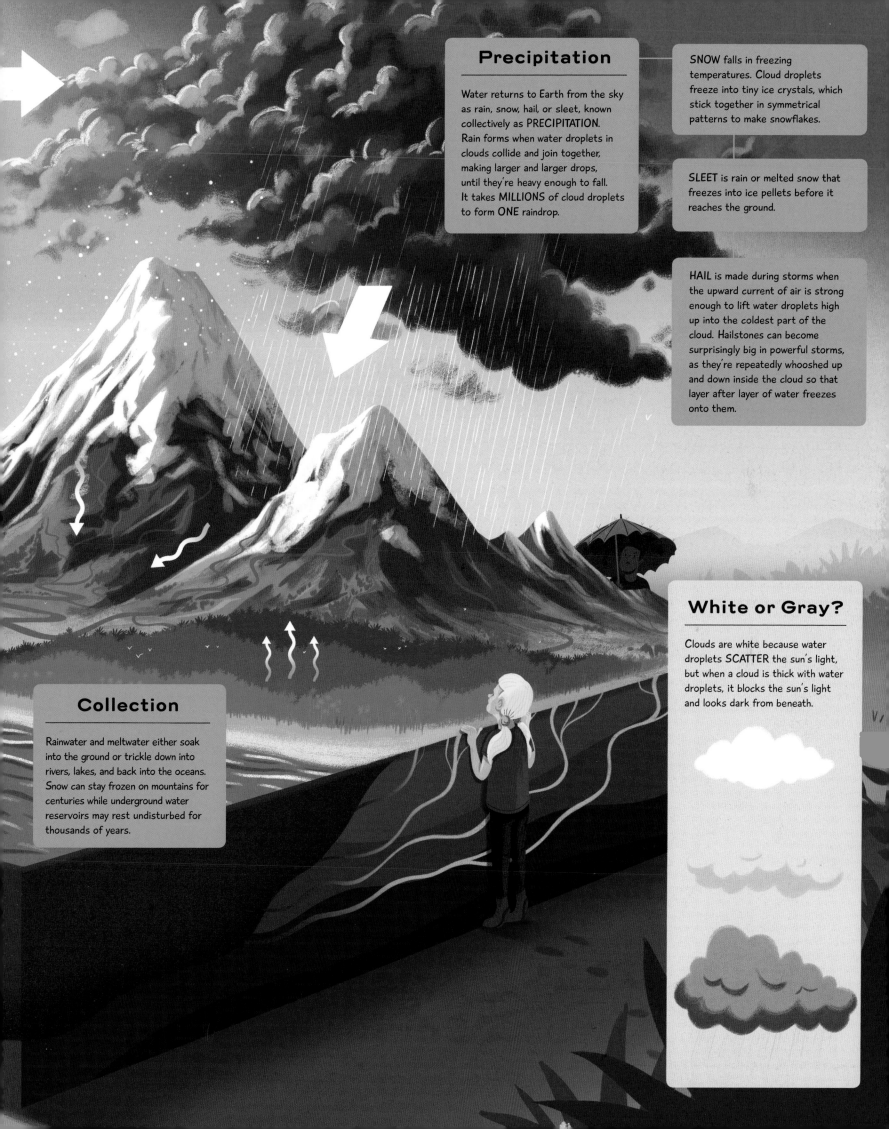

## Precipitation

Water returns to Earth from the sky as rain, snow, hail, or sleet, known collectively as PRECIPITATION. Rain forms when water droplets in clouds collide and join together, making larger and larger drops, until they're heavy enough to fall. It takes MILLIONS of cloud droplets to form ONE raindrop.

SNOW falls in freezing temperatures. Cloud droplets freeze into tiny ice crystals, which stick together in symmetrical patterns to make snowflakes.

SLEET is rain or melted snow that freezes into ice pellets before it reaches the ground.

HAIL is made during storms when the upward current of air is strong enough to lift water droplets high up into the coldest part of the cloud. Hailstones can become surprisingly big in powerful storms, as they're repeatedly whooshed up and down inside the cloud so that layer after layer of water freezes onto them.

## White or Gray?

Clouds are white because water droplets SCATTER the sun's light, but when a cloud is thick with water droplets, it blocks the sun's light and looks dark from beneath.

## Collection

Rainwater and meltwater either soak into the ground or trickle down into rivers, lakes, and back into the oceans. Snow can stay frozen on mountains for centuries while underground water reservoirs may rest undisturbed for thousands of years.

# Rivers

A river's journey can be very long and varied. Hundreds of explorers have set off on quests to seek out where a river begins, or to discover its final destination.

Over many thousands of years, rivers carve their own channels through the landscape, finding the best downhill paths through changing landscapes. They begin as trickling streams, running down from mountains and hills, pulled by the force of gravity. The streams join together to make small rivers, which in turn feed into large rivers. Finally, the big, broad rivers snake their way into large lakes or into the sea.

## 1. River Source

The SOURCE of a river is the point FARTHEST AWAY from where it ends. With many little streams feeding into a river, it's sometimes hard to locate the original. The starting point of a stream is usually a spring (water gushing up from underground), a marsh, a lake, or a glacier.

## 3. Glaciers

In cold mountainous regions, snow builds up over time. Every year, a new layer of snow covers the old layer, squashing down on it. Sometimes enough snow collects and is compacted to create a LARGE MASS OF ICE, known as a GLACIER. The glacier creeps slowly downhill, like a massive river of ice, carving out the ground beneath it and creating its own U-shaped valley.

## 2. Valleys

Valleys are the lower areas between mountains and hills, usually CARVED OUT BY WATER over many thousands of years. In mountainous areas, the water flows fast, eroding (wearing away) rock and cutting downward to create steep-sided, V-shaped valleys. Valleys between lower hills are broader and shallower.

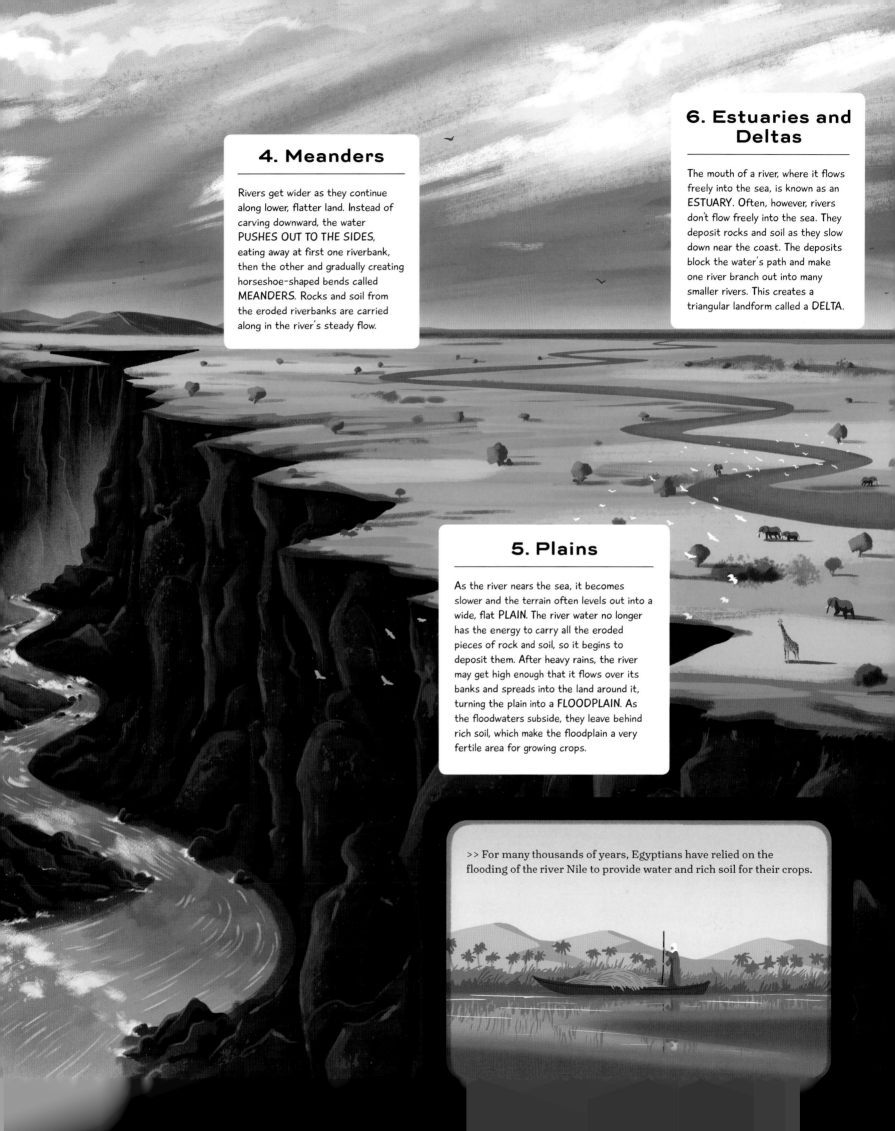

## 4. Meanders

Rivers get wider as they continue along lower, flatter land. Instead of carving downward, the water PUSHES OUT TO THE SIDES, eating away at first one riverbank, then the other and gradually creating horseshoe-shaped bends called MEANDERS. Rocks and soil from the eroded riverbanks are carried along in the river's steady flow.

## 6. Estuaries and Deltas

The mouth of a river, where it flows freely into the sea, is known as an ESTUARY. Often, however, rivers don't flow freely into the sea. They deposit rocks and soil as they slow down near the coast. The deposits block the water's path and make one river branch out into many smaller rivers. This creates a triangular landform called a DELTA.

## 5. Plains

As the river nears the sea, it becomes slower and the terrain often levels out into a wide, flat PLAIN. The river water no longer has the energy to carry all the eroded pieces of rock and soil, so it begins to deposit them. After heavy rains, the river may get high enough that it flows over its banks and spreads into the land around it, turning the plain into a FLOODPLAIN. As the floodwaters subside, they leave behind rich soil, which make the floodplain a very fertile area for growing crops.

>> For many thousands of years, Egyptians have relied on the flooding of the river Nile to provide water and rich soil for their crops.

# Coastlines

**Coastlines are the dramatic boundaries between ocean and land. They are continually being shaped by the power of the elements—and by our own attempts to conquer nature.**

There are hundreds of thousands of miles of coastline on Planet Earth, ranging from remote sandy beaches to busy harbors and from towering cliffs to long, low shingle spits. Almost half the world's population lives near the sea. Ports provide important transportation and trade links, while beaches are a magnet for vacationers and leisure activities. In fact, most of the world's biggest cities are built along the coast—and yet coastlines are one of the least stable regions on Earth.

## Bays and headlands

Waves pound rocky coastlines, gradually breaking up the rock into boulders, pebbles, shingle, and sand. Soft rock erodes the quickest, curving in to create bays between resistant headlands of harder rock. Sheltered by the headlands, the bays are filled in over time with deposits of fine sand.

## Making waves

Day in day out, WAVES lap and crash against our shores. Waves are ripples created by the wind blowing over the ocean. The size of the waves depends on the STRENGTH OF THE WIND and the DISTANCE the waves travel, known as their FETCH.

The stronger the wind and the greater the fetch, the bigger the waves become; so a storm far out at sea can result in huge waves reaching land. As waves reach shallow coastal waters, they're pushed up by the ground below to form steep crests, which come crashing down on the shore.

## Cliffs

Chalk, limestone, and sandstone are more resistant to EROSION and WEATHERING than other rock types. They stand tall and proud along the coastline, presenting a defiant, vertical cliff face to the mighty ocean. But even rock-solid cliffs don't last forever...

Caves are gradually undercut into the cliffs on prominent headlands.

They hollow out to create arches...

which eventually collapse to leave stacks...

...and slowly erode down into stumps.

## Tides

Twice a day the water level at the seaside falls and twice a day it rises. TIDAL MOVEMENT is caused by the MOON orbiting the Earth. The Moon's gravity PULLS on the ocean water, making tidal bulges either side of the globe. As the Earth spins, its shores pass in and out of the bulges, creating high and low tides.

**Low tide** is when the water level falls and lots of the beach is visible.

**High tide** is when the water level is high and covers more of the coastline.

## Exposing the past

The coast is a fabulous place to study the history of our planet. Ancient forests, swamps, deserts, plants, and animals have all been flattened and PRESERVED as layers of rock, or FOSSILS. These are hidden deep underground for millions of years, until the sea finally exposes their secrets.

# Tectonic Plates

**Earth is a massive ball of extremely hot metal and rock, with a thin, brittle outer shell. The shell has fractured over time to make a giant, spherical jigsaw of pieces, called tectonic plates.**

There are seven main plates and many smaller ones. They are resting on a layer of hot fluid-like rock. Heat currents rising from deep within the planet make the tectonic plates move—sometimes as far as 4 inches a year. This may not sound very impressive, but the consequences of massive plates of rock, millions of miles wide, slowly rubbing against each other or pulling apart, can be tremendous. People study plate tectonics to understand how mountains and trenches form, why earthquakes and volcanoes happen, and what dramatic events might occur in the near future...

## Pulling Apart

CONSTRUCTIVE BOUNDARIES, also known as divergent boundaries, are where plates PULL APART from each other (diverge) and magma RISES UP from beneath the lithosphere to create new plate material. These boundaries usually occur on the ocean floor, opening up deep ocean rifts.

Occasionally constructive boundaries occur between two continental plate boundaries and wrench the land apart. For example, the African plate pulling away from the Arabian plate formed a vast rift—which became the Red Sea!

## Plate Boundaries

This map shows the world's main tectonic plates and the boundary lines where they meet. Arrows indicate the direction the plates are moving in. There are THREE TYPES of plate boundaries: constructive, destructive, and transform boundaries.

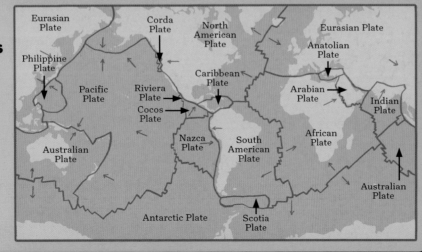

Eurasian Plate
Corda Plate
North American Plate
Eurasian Plate
Philippine Plate
Anatolian Plate
Pacific Plate
Riviera Plate
Caribbean Plate
Arabian Plate
Cocos Plate
Indian Plate
Nazca Plate
South American Plate
African Plate
Australian Plate
Australian Plate
Antarctic Plate
Scotia Plate

## Sliding Past

TRANSFORM BOUNDARIES are where plates slide alongside each other. No plate material is added or lost, but there's often great friction and a buildup of tension, which can result in devastating earthquakes.

## Earth's Layers

**Crust**—the thin outer layer

Sea

Land

**Mantle**— the very thick layer between Earth's core and its crust

**Lithosphere**— the crust and the top layer of the mantle combined

**Outer core**—this part of the Earth's core is liquid rather than solid.

**Inner core**— the innermost area of planet Earth

## Pushing Together

DESTRUCTIVE BOUNDARIES, or convergent boundaries, are where two plates PUSH TOGETHER (converge) and plate material is destroyed. The Earth's crust may crumple up, creating mountains, or buckle down, forming a sea trench. One plate usually ends up being forced under the other, where it melts and becomes magma. Oceanic crust is thinner and heavier than continental crust, so when these two meet, it's the oceanic crust which is forced underneath.

Himalayas

Tibetan plate

Eurasian plate

Indian plate

The highest mountain range in the world, the Himalayas, began to form 50 million years ago, when the Indian and Eurasian plates collided. The plates are still pushing together today and the mountains are still growing taller—at a rate of up to 7 mm a year.

# Earthquakes

Have you ever experienced an earthquake? It's possible you have without even realizing it. Each year, millions of earthquakes take place on Earth. Around 100,000 are strong enough to be felt, and just a hundred or so cause any damage. Only one is likely to be so violent that it causes a major disaster.

An earthquake is a sudden shaking of the ground, caused by movement deep within the Earth. Earthquakes are most common near plate boundaries, where two tectonic plates can get stuck as they move past each other and pressure can build up. When the plates finally break free, the sudden release of pressure sends vibrations, known as tremors, through the Earth's crust. Violent tremors destroy buildings and scar the land. They come with no warning and they are a serious danger to all living things.

## Earthquake Advice

If you're unlucky enough to experience an earthquake, here's what you should do to KEEP SAFE:

DROP — COVER — HOLD ON

DROP—Drop down to the floor.

COVER—Take cover, for example crawl under a sturdy table.

HOLD ON—Hold on (e.g., to the table legs) until the shaking stops.

## Inside an Earthquake

**Epicenter**—the area on the Earth's surface directly above the earthquake, where the shaking is at its most powerful.

**Shock waves**—waves of energy rippling out from the epicenter, getting weaker the farther they go, but still causing shaking and damage.

**Focus**—the earthquake's starting point, deep underground, where pressure is suddenly released.

## Underground Clues

Scientists study earthquakes to learn more about the insides of the Earth. The FOCUS of an earthquake can be over 60 miles under the ground—far deeper than we could ever explore. As SHOCK WAVES travel through the Earth, they speed up and slow down depending on how solid the material is that it's traveling through. Scientists use this information to figure out what the world is made of.

## Strength

Minor earthquakes feel a bit like a long rumble of thunder. They make the things around you vibrate. Major earthquakes feel like a sudden jolt. They're followed quickly by strong shaking.

Scientists figure out how strong an earthquake is by measuring the vibrations with a machine called a SEISMOMETER. They use a scale—the RICHTER SCALE—to rate the earthquake strength from 1 to 10. Each increase of 1 on the scale means the vibrations are 10 times greater.

## Tsunamis

When the epicenter of an earthquake is on the ocean floor, the shock waves can travel across the ocean as FAST AS A JET PLANE, in a series of giant waves.

As the waves reach the shore, the shallow water pushes them up to heights of 100 feet or more—about as tall as a 10-story building. These waves, or TSUNAMIS, can travel up to 10 miles inland, destroying much of what lies in their path.

Plate     Plate

Epicenter

# Volcanoes

**From steady streams of sizzling lava to sudden explosions of ash, gas, and magma, volcanoes remind us that the ground deep beneath us is far from stable.**

Beneath the Earth's crust is a mass of extremely hot, solid rock, known as the mantle. It's kept solid by the intense pressure around it, but sometimes the pressure is released and liquid rock escapes up through the Earth's crust in volcanoes. When magma reaches the Earth's surface, it's called lava.

Most volcanoes occur at plate boundaries, where tectonic plates rub against each other. Active volcanoes are ones that have erupted in the last 10,000 years and are likely to erupt again. In long periods between eruptions, they're described as dormant. Extinct volcanoes are ones that have been out of action for over 10,000 years and are unlikely to erupt again.

## Hot Spots

Away from plate boundaries, a volcano can form above a HOT SPOT, where a plume of magma, hotter than the surrounding area, rises up and ERUPTS through the Earth's crust. Hot spots remain in the same place, but the Earth's crust doesn't, so over time a chain of volcanic islands can develop. The one farthest from the hot spot is the oldest.

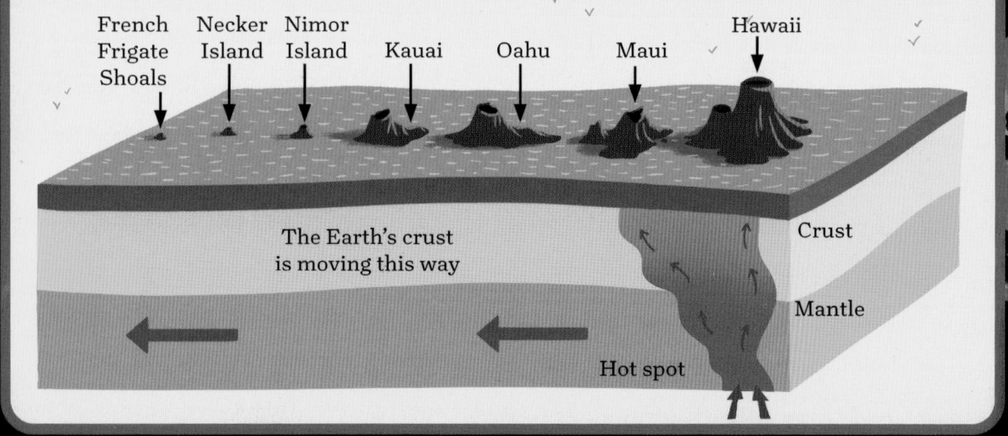

French Frigate Shoals — Necker Island — Nimor Island — Kauai — Oahu — Maui — Hawaii

The Earth's crust is moving this way

Crust

Mantle

Hot spot

## Deadly Ash

When Mount Vesuvius erupted in southern Italy in AD 79, vast quantities of volcanic rock and ash wiped out the Roman city of Pompeii and its 2,000 inhabitants. A writer called PLINY THE YOUNGER described the event in great detail, lending his name to that type of eruption. The layers of debris have preserved the town to this day.

## Stratovolcano

This cone-shaped volcano is a STRATOVOLCANO or composite volcano. It's built up (composed) over time from layers (strata) of lava, ash, and other materials, spewed out by consecutive eruptions.

The channel and opening created by the magma is known as a VOLCANIC VENT. Some volcanoes have a crater at the center, which forms when a pool of trapped magma builds up underground and eventually blasts out, creating a massive hole.

## Volcano Types

All volcanoes are openings in the Earth's surface, but they occur for different reasons. Here are the main types of volcano.

STRATOVOLCANOES form in destructive zones, where tectonic plates push together.

SHIELD VOLCANOES are low volcanoes that form in constructive zones, where tectonic plates pull apart.

FISSURE ERUPTIONS occur along long fractures in the Earth's crust, where magma spurts up in a line creating a curtain of fire.

SPATTER CONES are low volcanoes with steep sides. They form when magma erupts in big blobs that fall close to the vent.

PLINIAN or VESUVIAN ERUPTIONS are particularly powerful and spew a tall column of gas and ash into the air.

# Mountains

Are you ready to explore some of the coldest and most challenging places on Earth? You'll need the latest climbing equipment, thermal underwear, and months of hard training. Even then you might not make it to the top. Avalanches, blizzards, thick fog, and freezing temperatures are just a few of the obstacles you might meet...

The higher up a mountain you go, the colder it gets. In fact, there's a drop of up to 5 degrees Fahrenheit for every 1,000-foot increase in height. As a result, the same mountain can have several distinct ecosystems, with different plants and animals adapting to the different conditions. Mountains even make their own weather—they force air up and over them, so that the air cools and condenses into rain clouds, and suddenly you're in for a storm!

## Rain Shadow

Mountains tend to have a WET SIDE and a DRY SIDE. The wet side is the side the wind usually comes from. Moist air is blown toward the mountain and pushed up until it falls as rain.

The mountain blocks rain from reaching the opposite side, resulting in a dry area known as a RAIN SHADOW. The Death Valley desert in the USA is the hottest place on Earth, and one of the driest, because it's in the rain shadow of the Sierra Nevada mountain range.

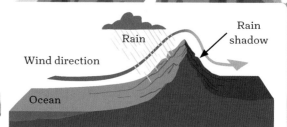

Rain

Rain shadow

Wind direction

Ocean

## How High?

The planet's highest mountain above sea level is MOUNT EVEREST in the Himalayas. It reaches up over 5 miles into the sky (29,000 feet)!

If you count below sea level as well, then the tallest mountain on Earth is the volcano MAUNA KEA on the island of Hawaii. It's 6 miles high from top to bottom, but most of the mountain is hidden under the sea.

**Mount Everest**
Height: 29,000 ft

**Mauna Kea**
Total height: 33,500 ft

13,800 above sea level

19,700 ft below sea level

## Safe Haven

What makes the mountains treacherous and uninhabitable for some also makes them a safe haven for others. Wild goats such as the ibex choose to bring up their young on near-vertical rock faces. They are so nimble and sure-footed that they manage to outrun mountains wolves and foxes who are looking for their next meal. Peregrine falcons choose to nest on high crags that are almost impossible to reach, to keep their eggs and chicks safe from predators.

## Above the Tree Line

Mountains tend to be surrounded by a frill of trees. The place where the trees stop growing and the bare mountainside begins is known as the TREE LINE.

Above this line, the harsher mountain environment begins and only low-lying shrubs can survive. Winds become more powerful, the air turns cooler and on a clear day the views stretch out for miles.

## Making Mountains

Mountains are created by the movement of the Earth's tectonic plates. There are five main types of mountains.

**VOLCANIC MOUNTAINS** form when volcanoes erupt. Molten rock (lava) spews out of the volcano. It cools and turns into layer upon layer of rock that builds up into a high peak. Famous examples include Kilimanjaro in Tanzania and Mount Fuji in Japan.

**FOLD MOUNTAINS** form when tectonic plates smash against each other and the Earth's crust buckles up in giant folds. The longest mountain ranges in the world are made of folded crust, with the Andes in South America being the longest at over 4,500 miles.

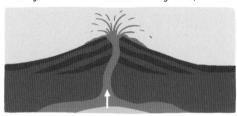

**BLOCK MOUNTAINS** form when huge blocks of rock shift up next to a fault line—a long crack in the surface of the Earth's surface. The Sierra Nevada mountain range in the USA is a good example.

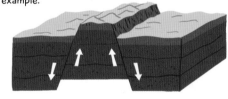

**DOME MOUNTAINS** form when magma bulges up beneath the Earth's crust but never breaks through to the surface. They often have descriptive names, such as the Pyramid and Enchanted Rock.

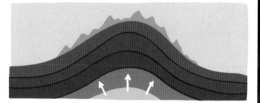

**PLATEAU MOUNTAINS** form when streams and rivers carve deep channels into a large, flat area of rock (a plateau). The channels become valleys and the high ground in between becomes plateau mountains.

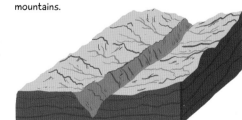

# Human Impact

**People have only been around for a tiny fraction of Earth's history (200,000 years out of 4.5 billion) but in that time we have changed the face of the planet.**

Two hundred years ago, there were one billion people on Earth. Now there are over seven billion. Surprisingly, we only live on less than 3% of Earth's land surface, but our actions have left their mark on over 80% of it, and on Earth's oceans and atmosphere too.

## Forests

Planet Earth has lost over half its trees since humans came along and started cutting them down to provide wood for fuel and open spaces for farming, villages, and towns. Forests now cover LESS THAN A THIRD of the planet's land surface and they're still being destroyed today. It's not just the trees we're losing, but the animals and plants that live in forested areas too.

## Towns and Cities

If you looked down at Earth from space at night, you'd see it sprinkled with lights. OVER HALF the world's population lives in urban areas. There are now 37 MEGACITIES on Earth—cities with over 10 million inhabitants—and counting.

Vast networks of roads and railways connect our towns and cities, crisscrossing countries and continents. Meanwhile the skies are humming with aircraft, with over 5,000 planes above the United States alone at any one time. Exhaust fumes from vehicles mingle with the air we breathe and add greenhouse gases to the atmosphere.

## Raw Materials

The things we build, the fuel we burn, and the products we buy start off as RAW MATERIALS from the natural world. Plastic comes from oil, paper and cardboard come from wood, bricks are made from clay, and so on. Trees can be planted again but most raw materials can't be replaced. The FOSSIL FUELS— coal, oil, and natural gas—have formed over millions of years. They're known as NON-RENEWABLE because they cannot be replaced, at least not in the next million years. If we keep using up the planet's natural resources, we'll have to live very differently in the future—or start raiding other planets for their resources instead.

## Farming

Much of the countryside we know today is actually MAN-MADE. The fields and hedgerows, crops, and farm animals were all put there by people. Although farming has been going on for thousands of years, modern methods are particularly harmful to the land.

Larger fields, crop spraying, and heavy machinery all play a part in destroying natural wildlife. But more humans on Earth mean more mouths to feed, so growing enough food while preserving the planet is a tricky undertaking.

## Positive Impact

People can also have a positive impact on the planet and work to improve the world around us. Here are some examples:

Old quarries can be turned into nature reserves.

Animals at risk of extinction can be protected and looked after until they can survive in the wild again.

People can plant more trees and wild meadows and hedgerows.

New technology and ideas can stop people from burning fossil fuels and creating harmful exhaust fumes.

Can you think of any ways to have a positive impact on the world around you?

# Pollution

**Humans create an awful lot of waste. Think of what you've thrown in the trash and flushed down the toilet today. Add the exhaust fumes from any vehicles you've been in. Then there are the gases given off to heat your home and your water, and to make the electricity you use...**

Pollution is what happens to the natural world around us when it's dirtied by waste, chemicals, and other harmful substances. Not all waste is harmful, and there are safe ways of dealing with it, but the more waste we produce, the harder it is to control and the more harm we are doing to our planet.

## Air Pollution

Factories, power stations, road vehicles, and fires all release waste gases that POLLUTE the air. It's harder for animals and people to breathe when the air is polluted.

Some of these waste gases thicken the atmosphere and trap more of the Sun's heat, causing the world to warm up. They can also combine with water droplets in the air and fall as a type of rain that's harmful to trees and fish, known as ACID RAIN.

## Garbage

Most of our trash is either burned or buried, but burning it gives off nasty fumes and we're running out of places to bury it. The biggest problem is PLASTIC.

It takes hundreds of years for a plastic bottle to break down and become part of the soil. Much of our plastic waste finds its way into streams, rivers, and oceans, where it can trap and kill wildlife. The best solution is to USE LESS plastic and to RECYCLE any plastic we do use.

## Water Pollution

The waste we flush down the toilet is known as SEWAGE. If it's treated properly then fresh water can be returned safely to the rivers and oceans. But untreated sewage causes water pollution and spreads disease.

Other major causes of water pollution are harmful chemicals from factories and farms, as well as carbon dioxide gas from the air that's absorbed by the oceans.

>> Before

>> After

Large areas of beautiful coral reefs are dying because pollutants are making the oceans more acidic.

## Keeping Positive

It's not all doom and gloom. Humans may be responsible for all kinds of pollution, but it doesn't have to be this way. The more we know about how we're harming the planet, the more we can change our habits and make the planet a better place in the future. Turn the page to find out how!

# Saving Planet Earth

Earth is our home—and it's the only planet in our solar system where life flourishes. It needs to be respected and protected so that life can thrive for millions more years.

To do this, we need to move away from burning fossil fuels and belching gases into the atmosphere. We need to preserve the planet's natural resources by replacing or recycling the raw materials we use. We need to protect natural habitats and give wildlife its own space to live. Crucially, we need to work together, with countries all around the world agreeing to laws to safeguard the planet. It's a difficult task, but it's not impossible.

## Cleaner, Greener Energy

We don't have to burn coal and oil to create electricity and to power our vehicles. There are many alternative sources of energy—the Sun, the wind, the rise and fall of the tide, the rush of a river. These don't create pollution and they're RENEWABLE, which means they won't run out!

**Green walls**, also known as living walls, are covered in plants. They create more living space for wildlife, as well as insulating the rooms inside.

## Lifestyle Changes

Small changes in your daily life can help reduce the amount of pollution you create.

Try walking or cycling instead of taking the bus or traveling by car.

Visit the local seaside rather than flying abroad.

Buy food that's been grown on farms near you, to reduce the fumes created by transporting it.

Put a sweater on instead of turning up the heating.

Buy your clothes from a secondhand store.

You might think these changes won't make a difference, but imagine if everyone on the planet did the same. That really would change the world!

**Tidal barriers** use the movement of water to generate electricity.

**Recycle** here!

Buying **secondhand** items saves money and reduces waste.

Garden and kitchen waste can be used to make **compost**—food that helps new plants to grow.

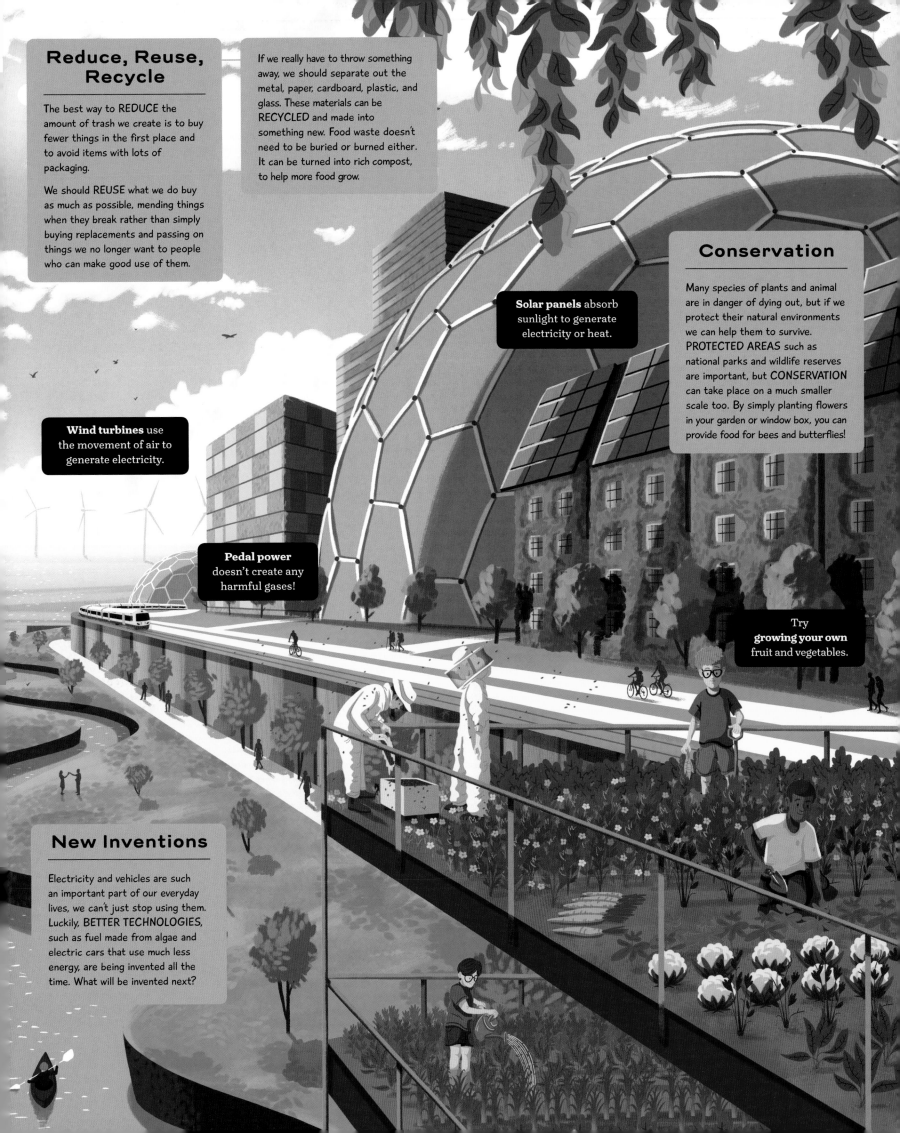

## Reduce, Reuse, Recycle

The best way to REDUCE the amount of trash we create is to buy fewer things in the first place and to avoid items with lots of packaging.

We should REUSE what we do buy as much as possible, mending things when they break rather than simply buying replacements and passing on things we no longer want to people who can make good use of them.

If we really have to throw something away, we should separate out the metal, paper, cardboard, plastic, and glass. These materials can be RECYCLED and made into something new. Food waste doesn't need to be buried or burned either. It can be turned into rich compost, to help more food grow.

## Conservation

Many species of plants and animal are in danger of dying out, but if we protect their natural environments we can help them to survive. PROTECTED AREAS such as national parks and wildlife reserves are important, but CONSERVATION can take place on a much smaller scale too. By simply planting flowers in your garden or window box, you can provide food for bees and butterflies!

**Solar panels** absorb sunlight to generate electricity or heat.

**Wind turbines** use the movement of air to generate electricity.

**Pedal power** doesn't create any harmful gases!

Try **growing your own** fruit and vegetables.

## New Inventions

Electricity and vehicles are such an important part of our everyday lives, we can't just stop using them. Luckily, BETTER TECHNOLOGIES, such as fuel made from algae and electric cars that use much less energy, are being invented all the time. What will be invented next?

Brimming with creative inspiration, how-to projects, and useful information to enrich your everyday life, Quarto Knows is a favorite destination for those pursuing their interests and passions. Visit our site and dig deeper with our books into your area of interest: Quarto Creates, Quarto Cooks, Quarto Homes, Quarto Lives, Quarto Drives, Quarto Explores, Quarto Gifts, or Quarto Kids.

Text © 2018 Quarto Publishing plc.
Illustrations © 2018 Tom Clohosy Cole.
Written by Jo Nelson.

First Published in 2018 by Wide Eyed Editions, an imprint of The Quarto Group.
400 First Avenue North, Suite 400, Minneapolis, MN 55401, USA.
T (612) 344-8100 F (612) 344-8692 www.QuartoKnows.com

ISBN 978-1-78603-062-7

The illustrations were created digitally.
Set in Trio Grotesk, Turnip, and Playtime With Hot Toddy

Published by Jenny Broom and Rachel Williams
Designed by Nicola Price
Edited by Kate Davies
Production by Jenny Cundill

Manufactured in Dongguan, China TL1117

9 8 7 6 5 4 3 2 1